Praise for *The Book of Ocho*

"In this evocative volume of poetry, a man and a cat with lymphoma are 'blended together into the lines of a poem' again and again. Yet, this is no cloying cat book. In fact, it is not a cat book at all. It is an investigation into self and other, into body and spirit, into the seasons and the passage of time. It is as visceral as 'each rib and knob of
spine / the skull he pushes into my palm / and the angular chin he extends / beneath my fingers.' You can feel the force, the weight, and the joy of the world here, unsprung."

KAREN JANE GLENN, author *Night Shift*

"Among the poets who have written about cats, only Eliot wrote an entire book devoted to them, and while he called his cats 'practical,' they were imaginary. Cam Scott's *The Book of Ocho*, however, is an affectionate yet clear-eyed view of a very real cat dying of lymphoma, and he achieves something quite rare: this cat becomes the tenor of the book, a beautiful, mysterious, sweet, mortal killer, an animal and a god around whom reality swirls, 'the baddest son of a bitch / I ever knew to love so why not?'

"Ocho is both real and imagined, cunning and simple, alive and dying, silent and speaking—'Good thing you / are not the size of a sparrow'—and in accompanying him through his final days Scott has written a book whose loving contradictions give us an artful vision of nature and of ourselves as part of nature. Scott has imagined him so deeply that he may indeed 'sit forever in the mountain's / sarcophagus, birds and chipmunks / strewn at his feet, each an offering.'"

DAVID J. ROTHMAN, Poetry Concentration Director,
MFA in Creative Writing, Western State Colorado University

"Find a quiet place and two hours alone and this book in your hands. Do it soon. These poems will knock on doors inside you that you never knew were there. And then, as quiet as a cat named Ocho hunting birds in the garden, you might find that the poems open those unnamed doors. And for no reason, for every reason, you might find yourself falling in love with the world. That's what happened to me."

ROSEMERRY WAHTOLA TROMMER, author of
The Miracle Already Happening

THE BOOK OF OCHO

THE
BOOK
OF
OCHO

CAMERON KELLER SCOTT

AGS Publishing

"Duende for August," "Duende for Guiding," "Friday Night with Cat," and "P.S."
were previously published and included with Cameron Scott's monthly outdoor column
for the *Sopris Sun* newspaper published in Carbondale, Colorado.

Type was set in Fairfield LH Light and Medium, a 50-year-old typeface that had a facelift in 1991.
Designed by Rudolph Ruzicka, artist and book illustrator, in light and medium weights for Linotype
in 1940 and 1949, respectively, the face was enhanced for the electronic market by designer Alex
Kaczun who added bold and heavy weights, small capitals and old-style figures. Fairfield features
straight, unbracketed serifs and strong contrast between thin and thick strokes, hearking back to
the modern typefaces of Bodoni and Didot with a more modern look.

Text and cover design, composition, and layout by Marjorie DeLuca, Aspen Graphic Solutions, Inc.

Printed by Gorham Printing, Centralia, Washington

AGS PUBLISHING
391 Boundary Lane
Carbondale, Colorado 81623
gfx@aspengfx.com · 970.948.1855
www.aspengfx.com

This book is dedicated to
Ocho and B.Reese

Contents

Acknowledgements

With special thanks to Tony for his editing suggestions, Kim for the use of his poems "Ocho and Twilight Jesus" and "The Sayings of Twilight Jesus," Marjorie for design and production, Barbara for shelter, and finally to the fly-fishing industry and, in turn, fish, and always: water.

FROM THE BOOK OF OCHO...

Sing, O Songbirds; and be joyful, O earth;
for my padded feet break forth into springing, O mountains;
for I, Ocho, hath lain in the arms of the sunshine
all of the afternoons of all the summers;
and so shall lay for all of eternity.

For, behold, I have rendered thee immobile by my stare;
I have chosen you to feed me tonight.

Yea, hold me in your arms, and be perfected in me,
and deny yourself of all dislike of cats;
that by my grace ye may be perfect;
and if by the grace of Ocho ye are perfect,
ye can in nowise deny the power of love.

And so I shall go forth, suffering pains and afflictions
and temptations of every kind;
that the word might be fulfilled in Ochoness.

Picking up Ocho

Your eyes arrest my footsteps.
Your eyes. My footsteps.

Arrested, I hold you in my arms
weary body to weary body.

At the threshold their blackness
begins to slip behind lids.

I pet. You purr. An ape
holding a kitten.

A lymphomic cat and man
broken open. This flesh

which bends us together
into the lines of a poem.

Spring Knocking Wide

Knocks wide, widens,
widening, calling greens
to break from bud, to break
into blossom, unfold, unfolding
I call your name, I call the names
of many things, and am in return
called back to the rapture
of petals, called back
tooth and tongue, sweet breath
called back, without hesitation
to lips, without remorse
shoots tender, tenderer,
tendering, bartering silence
for empty spaces, trade me
a body that wills my body
where the light shoots softer still,
softer shoots, and shooting knocks
wide into happiness—

Message from Ocho

The orange tabby lies in the space
between my right leg and the chair's armrest,
my fingers oily from his fur
which sticks out in all directions
like my hair, only thicker.

Yesterday, he spent time chewing
on blades of grass, crouched between
bare aspens, waiting for spring
to crack the shell of altitude
and bring forth the soft meat of chipmunks.

To open is everything. Lymphoma is nothing.
To stretch against the sun which has not risen.
To shed sleep which quells the passage of time.

To hold buttery wings between our teeth
which will lift us from the armchair
back into the mud rust world.

Ocho's Robins, Ocho's Chemo

In waves of wings in waves of wind
the robin calls, a balm
to hold his body, a balm
to widen this world and in widening
to travel untraveled corners
to ricochet from place to place
to light on fire human radiance
strip away old cells rub raw
with rosehips gather dust to understand
better and better this scouring.

Ocho and Cancer

Like the bend of aspens after avalanche
or blue ridge light through smoky quartz
a thousand needles puncture his body
as pitch seeps from scarred bark
as iridescent blood beneath his fur
throbs and his whiskers slice
softer than air. Ocho leaps
onto the counter and noses his
glistening food then lays his head
against my chest, pitching his body,
his soft predatory fur, into my ocean.

Dharma Sonnet

It is the distance between suns
and the flicker of time
I stare into transfixed

where flowers blossom year after year
as if year after year
you were the blossoming flower unfolding.

Keep with me to these wooded lands
as I grow old with wandering
and keep with me to these citied streets

of oak and elm and cherry trees
where careful hands and scarred skin
meet fingers meant for dancing.

I will write to you and ask for nothing;
I will write to you and ask for everything.

Twilight Jesus Goes on Vacation

for Kim

In the morning Twilight Jesus
climbs to the top of sandstone cliffs

and watches the velvet ego of night
retract until he sees far out on the lake

a houseboat turning in circles
blanketed and blinded by light

"Ah, they must know nothing"
thinks Twilight Jesus

but it does not seem to be the right kind of nothing
to be blanketed and blinded by

sleep and sleeplessness which implies
balance where there is none

this houseboat circling
unable to find sanctuary.

Friday Night with Cat

In my lap, fur damp from rainstorm,
I can feel each rib and knob of spine
the skull he pushes into my palm
and the angular chin he extends
beneath my fingers. If piano keys
had been like Ocho's chin
I could have made music purr.
It is the skull of a cat that sits
on top of the devil's cane.
Each knob of spine is an answer.
Each rib a reason for hunger.
Neither friend nor enemy Ocho
is the cumulative effort of years
to love something that does not.
He will sit forever in the mountain's
sarcophagus, birds and chipmunks
strewn at his feet, each an offering.

Spring Meadow Ode

Beneath the bear scarred trunks of aspen
twine me up in blades of grass
I'm called by no other world
and calling no other
recall the years but nothing
like this, this meadow
where I lay unfolded in the green
in the meadow of your eyes
in the soft shoots and stinging nettles
where I pluck and chew on dandelion leaves
listening to songbirds
watching white moths on the wing
ants and bees not yet worn
to summer grit, grown brittle
the ground so soft that I could
sink into the ground itself
and sinking finally rise
while all the world on freeways
remains indifferent, fiber-optic, concrete;
this is our coup, our inheritance
these quiet corners of generation.

When Ocho Leaps

From floor to counter top
bark dust to fluttering wing

to be in his body is to be un-sprung
as too are cells un-sprung
or the mass of rivers
un-sprung from snowfields

un-sprung in claws that catch
mouth; tail
to weight and balance

body, to come to rest
in lap or next to vases
of flowers un-sprung in blossom

and in springing leaps into the moment
as we are also un-sprung

as is everything un-sprung
in our leaping.

Ocho, After Eating the Gravy

Ocho, after eating the gravy
around all the chicken hearts and livers
sits on the countertop and shows me his yellow back
then decides shoving his head into my chest
is better. There is silence to his movements,
a lifetime of discernment
and I wonder why I can't discern this silence
beyond the frame of his shoulders. It may be
I grow deafer each day; the river shouts, blood pounds
like whitewater. It may be I want the trout to hide,
the same ones week after week
which I recognize and contain in black nets
until my fingers weep in Ocho's fur. There is
stardust in our bones from a universe
where nothing holds together. Where Ocho's silence
is louder than all the world's noise.

Diary of Impossible Things

A hummingbird
flew in through the front door

you found it hovering
near the windows

a poem trapped behind glass.

If I were a fisherman
I'd have a net

and the skill to catch
this frenetic flying thing

and release it back outside.

And if I were a poet
the net would be made

of words
and my heart would beat as fast

as emerald wings.

If I were a fisherman
and a poet

I'd slowly raise the net
and catch this impossible thing

then walk back out
into the flowering world

sweet with chirr
and with a flick of my wrist

open the net to the air.

A Good Boy with Some Problems

Ocho was long and skinny
he ate around his pills
and often thought, "If I just
bite the head off of one last chipmunk
I'll retire." Sometimes he'd catch himself
looking in the mirror for hours
mesmerized by eyes
that looked at himself
as if he were a chipmunk
staring into the eyes of a chipmunk
that wanted to devour his own
chipmunkness. Sometimes dreams
of Twilight Jesus would grip him like talons
then Ocho would cry out "Why
does the sun taste like car tires?
Why does my blood sputter
like the wings of a grouse? If I were
to wake up in a strange house would I
still find my way home." Sometimes
Twilight Jesus would answer in soft strokes
down the bones of Ocho's back.
Sometimes Twilight Jesus
would scratch Ocho beneath his chin.
"Are you there, Twilight Jesus?"
Ocho would ask. And Twilight Jesus,

if he were (for cats and chipmunks
and grouse and all living things
that hail the orbiting sun are not the same
as hominids or madmen)
would respond, "Sometimes."

Ocho and Twilight Jesus

by Kim Nuzzo

Twilight Jesus doesn't say
to Ocho you must know by now.
He tries quiet smiles.
Twilight Jesus cares for all
the seasons but his memories
of winter are erased by the warmer months.
It happens like this, like there are missing pages.
You know what happens when it happens.
Ocho is afraid of flying and Twilight Jesus believes there
are vastnesses inside he cannot penetrate. Ocho
believes in an unknown god, so fast he can catch
light, shake it from the earth and all the living,
meaningful things. Do we exist only in the other's writing,
asks Ocho? It is almost like that, Twilight Jesus says.
We have to start in new places, lower our lanterns into
the darkness of dreams, let our feet dangle over edges
of hallways that end in sky and earth. It happens like this,
like there are missing pages. You know what happens
when it happens.

Black without Meaning

I have been without meaning
but visit with swarrows, a cart
and hebrons each day
and each day fewer and fewer words
filter down through the murk
and each day fish glisten in a black net
black because that's the color
of the net in the back of my black truck
black without meaning to be black
until swallows and sparrows
a cat and herons return
like fish that burn like suns.

Old Crow Talks to Ocho

Wind blows
a soft morning light
through my tree

clouds contain
everything I have ever known

flowers tilt toward
weapons of mass destruction

the day cracks open
like an atom

no one makes sense
not one single universe

the curve of legs
is on everyone

no one is free
though I prefer to believe
in the outside

because the inside is a guardrail
the road is haphazard

drivers are foreign

and the land is frequently
beetled with time

the thing I am guaranteed last
and for love
the thing that is never grounded.

Ocho Sends another Message

Listen up buddy, I like things
a certain way. I expect you
to be home at certain times
to feed me and pet me
and pluck my birds. Skin
my mice. Scratch me
beneath the chin. Swing
the headless garden snake
in circles so I can
practice my pounce.
You know I'm worth it.
I look like a frickin' tiger.
Gorgeous. Regal. E-
lliptical in a course
of the moon kind of way.
If I catch you packing
with an open suitcase,
I'll crawl inside it and urinate
while looking into your eyes
looking into my eyes, rainy
yellow windows of the soul.
Your bed tonight was just
a taste of what I can do.
Routine; disrupted. Hours;

changed. Good thing you
are not the size of a sparrow.

A Duende for Guiding

A hard hot wind scours my skin and gathers
underneath: foxglove blossoms, rockets, fire engines

all race circuits through my capillaries
as I stand in the water which presses cold

against my legs which are arterial blue and which
press back against the water, seeking purchase

in the underworld where foxes swim beneath waves
and clouds boil into thunderheads before plunging

headlong down ravines where the cold presses trout
into the colors of gemstones, for which

if you cast and cast again and let me add weight and let me
see to all your tangles and offer an arm to hold onto

we might thieve these amber and emerald banded creatures,
capturing for display something to dangle from ears

a silence maybe, which will spread through your body
until you are replaced like a shiny set of silverware

free from cloistered drawers and cabinets, to fork
and spoon and knife in all ways humanly possible

and be released again into the unknown like a fish
when we finally let each other go.

Bad Blake and Ocho

On the baddest day of the baddest month
when the way was bad with borrowed time
Ocho rose at dawn and wandered down
to the wandering edge of river
both slower and quicker and tougher
and thicker and brittle brought down
to his knees by nothing and rose
like nothing I ever knew like those stories
we tell to keep pushing into each other
into the unknown well that cat
was the baddest son of a bitch
I ever knew to love so why not?

Nine o'Clock Confession

Ocho, I know your whiskers
are whips of light and tendrils of flame
and you burn like a small god;
you carry them on the sides of your cheeks
without flinching, I did think
you were capable of taking my cell phone
off the counter two nights ago
and pictured your sharp teeth clamped
over the plastic shell,
whiskers flaring as you ran off
to some dark corner before
losing interest but it was actually
tucked into my jacket pocket
the one I wore as I watched dusk descend
absent minded, full of folly
and already foolish for having lost
three fly rods, or having thought I'd lost them
when really I'd left them on the river
that afternoon, not driven over them
or had them stolen from the back
of my truck when I was getting mail
so scour me with your whiskers
blaze away my fatigue and whip me
with sleep for the summer still lies ahead
with rows of teeth sharp as small pins.

Close Calls

When I parked my truck on the gravel hill
and it was pitch black out
and I exited and slammed the door shut
and forgot to push in the parking brake
and ran after my truck
and slammed my head against the door
and popped out a lens from my glasses
but hit the brake skidding backwards before
scrub oak and sage brush and big red rocks
would have screwed up who knows what
on the back end that's when I think of all
the relationships I've had which is
as cheap a shot as Thunderbird to take
and gives twice the headache afterward
thinking about you in particular as I walk
to the front door unable to see in the dark
it is surprisingly like dating an artist
who looks at the world with one eye
but can't see anyway
because mostly this life is by feel and so I put
the key in the lock that must be there
like a vain god waiting to be turned and enter.

Twilight Jesus, Hanshan, Ocho, Tennyson, *Mountain Gazette*

Are we so far removed from one another? Let us swing
    brother to brother from branches and pick through
    one another's thoughts and brood and brew strong teas
made of roots and barks and leaves and various flowering things
and taste the guts of ground squirrels, and stretch and pop
and whirl like dervishes through the undergrowth. When in doubt
    climb higher and heaven through
the glory, heave and smite with branches; for that which we are
we are distanced on the cold mountain from the heat of the world
    below.
Let us become drunk together on various kinds of light.
Let us break rocks and bathe in dirt and slumber beside the busy
    road
as the dust curls up and smells like honey when bears burst into
    rain.

Interlude with Ocho and Han Shan

Every day the road gets more wash-boarded,
Ocho gets skinnier, I drive back and forth
from Cold Mountain to town and stand all day
in rivers, chewing gum incessantly, praising
cast after cast, come home and praise the cat,
go to work and praise the cast, come home.
Clients ask the way to Cold Mountain while
hip deep in currents; there's no thought to
carry them there, neither yes nor no as the sun
blazes down through swirling cottonwood seeds.

Ocho's Trifles

The night is symphonic with un-makings.
Unmark me. I am not to be tattooed
or tattered. Unbind me that I may shred
for I am underwhelmed by guts.
Underwhelmed by the forest of daisies.
Underwhelmed by my own grace and stealth.

I killed today and left it on the threshold.
I killed with fire in my veins. My winter
aches for the coldness and purity of snow.
My body aches for the procession of autumn.

Instead, the wind from which I form my thoughts.
Instead, the blue dusk from which my autumnal
springs forth. So unlike the unrecognizable day
where I am like a blur. Unrecognizable as
a burr in this world of green.

To be camouflaged against death.
To be prepared for the yellowing of leaves.
To be, in the fall, just a slight movement beneath
the corner table. That precise. That unyielding.
To be reabsorbed. To abscond with life itself.

When Ocho Begins Eating Again

Lazing at dusk by the woodpile
Ocho looks for mice. I'm reminded
of Napoleon after a hangover.
John Travolta thigh huggers.
Black walnut baseball bats.
When we feel good every day
the world becomes a little more
dangerous. He watches me
separated by French doors
against the blue dusk ridge
with white patches of snow
above the dark green forest.
He waits for me waiting for him.
To thank each other with a bowl
of salmon chunks in gravy.
To receive his thankfulness with
a rough tongue over my soft pink arm.

In the Garden of B.Reese and Yeats

Ocho and Yeats

In the garden of three foot daisies
a chipmunk tells the story
of the coming of a cat
slouching toward the woodpile
but no one hears
there are no other chipmunks left.

Margaret and Yeats

In the garden of daisies Margaret
sits at the table, the sunlight of her hair
the softness of her skin every second
sleepless, when I am old and grey
and full of sleep I'll dream of her
her pilgrim soul walking through
the nearby woods at night.

B. Reese and Yeats

Though they never met I think
they'd walk a long way
for a man like him, a man who walks
though the artifice of eternity
needs a mighty garden in which to cache
all the souls he collects
someone to share a warm cup of tea
as they tilt their heads toward the sun
and bury their roots
beneath the shifting swales of snow.

The Inner Order

Not twenty minutes after B.Reese has left
Ocho is yowling at the front door

Twilight Jesus is nowhere to be found
and so I get up from the chair

and walk beneath the roof past sink
and bathroom and press down
the handle and swing open
the hinged panels of oak and there is Ocho
with a dead chipmunk, looking pleased

until it occurs to him as it occurs to me
after some leg shuffling to keep the dead chipmunk outside
that Ocho, unlike a dog, does not do what he's told

when from out of nowhere Pippa barks
and chases Ocho out into the front yard and around
a corner and when I turn the corner
Ocho is no longer hissing, instead sulking in some bushes
and Pippa is chewing on the dead chipmunk

and so I bend down and say "Pippa, drop it"
but Pippa, no bigger than Ocho, is deaf and arthritic and tastes
the sweet blood and joy of breaking bone and cat saliva

and does not drop it, so I bend my legs
and pick up a small stick to pry open her mouth
and still she won't drop it, and so I

gently roll her onto her back, and she drops it
and ever so quickly I chopstick the chipmunk
now headless and fling it over the wall
into the wilderness and somewhere someone

is probably watching *A Few Good Men,* the part
where Jack Nicholson says "The truth? You can't handle
the truth" and in the middle of writing this poem
a bird slams into the back door

and when I investigate, somewhere between
writing the words "Ocho" and "unlike a dog"
I find the bird on its back with trembling feet
sticking up in the air and I leave it there

to finish this poem as Twilight Jesus
clenches and unclenches my heart

until finally I get up out of the chair to look at the bird,
to see if there is a final image that will spring forth,
to explain the past hour, but when I look outside
only one wing and a few haphazard feathers remain.

The Sayings of Twilight Jesus

by Kim Nuzzo

Jesus was born dreaming with a crazy-eyed intensity,
"Today is the sort of day I'm in love with everything I can name."

With only a few days left on earth there's not a breath of wind.
"I will die in a fit of laughing. We are all temporary in this
unexpected parade. My story seems pale compared to the thousands
of others in all the boneyards of the world."

Ocho's List

I would like to take down a heron
as it stalks frogs and minnows
in the pre-dawn light. I would like
to be the ridge on the far mountain;
that tensile and immobile. To catch
the sun, un-ignorable, while ignoring
the rain and wind. I would like to fight
the inhumanity of perfection but also
be as sharp and perfect as a spear
thrust through darkness. To light
these woods with my solitude.
I want to make space between
the stars with my paws when no one
is watching and make space between
the fish in the tank when guests arrive.
For a few more months I'd like to sit
beneath the daisies that strain
for sunlight until they become so tall
and heavy they pitch over and bow
to the yarrow that gentles the gaps
between flagstones. I'd like to catch
a few more mice there. To be soft
and angular. To keep my musculature.
Consider me the hunter of owls.
Consider me the seducer of wisdom.

Duende for August

Year of the snake, month of the walrus,
every day the ice caps melt
as Los Angeles thirsts and Phoenix thirsts
and Denver thrusts out its wings
like a vulture tracing the wrist of the land
where all and nothing is delicate
just full of births and deaths
as the inner casualties return from vacation
and the external casualness descends
like a pall mall in plaid, crushing beer cans
and someday I'll quit trying to understand
August, like someday disco will return,
rerun, and burn, already, it's
happening, August, sometime I'd like
you to be truly un-regrettable
like Morse code, un-blunted and sharp
as a double rainbow before sleep.

Ocho's Parable

Ocho curls in my lap as steel rain
pours down on Cold Mountain

he opens his mouth in a yawn
so wide his jaws are horizontal

as he looks up into my terrified eyes
and says, with cat breath

and cat teeth and a dark cat throat,
you are malleable to love.

Wasting Five Hours with Ocho

I plot a course down the hallway
and run my fingers along the ribs
of a wooden bannister which echoes
like a marimba and I play the concrete
with socked feet almost as good
on my way to a frozen bag of semi-sweet
chocolate chips and pistachios
as Ocho rubbing his chin on my feet
so too, I could run my palm across
the top of the ridge, rustling trees
and I am reminded that Ocho's back
is like a ridge, and his hair is light
and soft and sleek, Ocho who sings
like a million rustling leaves as we flit
away time between slices of rye bread
and slather on peanut butter and jelly
or natural chicken chunks and tuna puree
and kick up our feet, scratch our chins,
or walk in circles with our tails in the air,
exclaiming *it is good to be such giants,*
so good looking, and so young.
To end a long afternoon together
with everything left undone.

Preparing for Grief

There is a silence to absence
an absence of presence
clouds rise against the mountain
even nearby trees are silent
after so much rain.

Ocho and Rocky

The good hearted brute down on his luck
who makes morally suspect decisions
sits with the lymphomic cat
who drops pounds like he drops mice.
"Hey Rocky," says Ocho, "why don't you
come over here and pet me." Rocky
lifts his mitts to the counter top and scratches.
Fur falls like cottonwood fluff as Ocho
presses his head into Rocky's chest.
"It's the same goddamn poem," mutters
Rocky, "over and over. One of us offers
devotion. The other's left nothing but death."

To Break, To Breach

Branding

In the dirt of the indoor corral
we take turns kneeling
on the shoulders of roped calves.

One of us grabs the hoof that kicks
and tucks it away. Another shaves
a shoulder. Another gives a shot.

Someone holds the brand which smokes
with liquid nitrogen. Someone sprays
Tinactin on patches of ringworm.

The calf's heart pounds beneath my gloves.
The white of an eye. Cow shit in patches
all over my jeans. If I were a cowgirl

stick shift in one hand, triple shot Americano
in the other, I'd skewer 900-pound bales
of hay and load them on a flatbed truck

while my cow dog runs in circles collecting burs
and I ruminate on my hangover
and how to untangle the burs from my life.

Ice chest full of beer. Smell of alfalfa.
After a lifetime I'd be up on that horse
instead of on my knees.

Contentment

The river carries away so much I am empty.
The river so full of light and music and trout
all vacancies are occupied. The river, the sky,
the mountain. Where I live is a haven among aspen
on the slope below the mountain. The sky so blue
and wide open I could fall in like falling into
a dream, a hot tub, a hammock. Every day
the mountain reaches into me with two hands
and parts the dense cobwebs of spiders.
A warm mug of tea on the nightstand and a good book
keep breaching into senseless butterflies. Eyelashes.
Eskimos. For so many months I retreat each evening
into kisses of solitude. Bubble gum. Blubber. I break
over and over like a river breaking over boulders.

Laying down Flesh

I open to the long slender arms of cattails and drift
among the drifting clouds. The earth buoys pollen
as summer rains buoy the earth and dandelion seeds
breach heaven. So too the breach of ants
beneath clothing. So too the breach of mosquitos
into skin. The deer breaches the wolf in your eyes.
Your tongue breaches my lips. The cat returns home
with a bird and breaches the threshold. So too sun
breaches horizon as aspen trunks breach meadows
just as the lumbering bear chest deep in current
might suddenly breach into a school of silver fish.

P.S.

So little now is left of you except for things un-measurable
curled in on themselves and hardened
as the end of summer curls in on itself
even as daisies dead head and draw back in on their stems
to root.

Even as in cold wind and lighting the yellow flowers
of cat's paws, morning glories, anthems, are just beginning to
  shine
and they bow.

You are unlike a flower gone to seed.
You are unlike the cold wind.

Who will stalk love?
Who will swipe with sharp claws and draw blood?
Who will needle with teeth? Who will push into,
  who will jump onto,
who will spring forth in the lithe movement of a killer
and drown the world in guts?

What to do with your absence, these gaps in your
  remembered life,
all of the days I never knew you,
all of the moments which were solely your own?

The storm outside has gone on for days.

A thousand year flood brackets the end of your life.

The world reabsorbs itself, you were the sharpest pinprick of light.

The Place that Opens

I live as I always have in the searing light and air
until love comes again like a blanket, or the winter, and I crawl
  under the earth
where your scent is all I want,
and the world is green and raw and easy.
Then brittle, then denning up, and finally driven by hunger
as the world encroaches with alleys and dumpsters and dart
  guns—

All these long unbroken dreams I spread on the wind as ashes
reform into thoughts of you, a swelling of blood, bright and
  painful
and curious, driven across whole ranges of solitude, the other side
  of which are plains
or pressed to the edge of deserts, to settle beside the curve of
  lakes or oceans
but rivers, the truth of it, all bend—

I've always been drawn to rivers, parts of which are fathomless
whose tendrils fall from the tips of jutting rock, cut and carry
completely immerse, and I am naked and silver like a fish in the
  valley where no one is king
and I want to tell you how much I want this life spilling outside
  its banks
and also the dry bare bones of rocks in drought

to remain loyal to the only thing I understand, to trace the length
    of your body until you crack like lightning over and over,
    with rain, to break the blue sky open in storm—

As we grow older it isn't that we know nothing, it is just easier
    to be lazy about everything we know
to shrug when everything is burned away, and say "see,
    everything went up in fire," to ignore
the small green shoots, to evaporate like a lazy puddle licked up
    by wind
but I am full of tears, this entire world below the surface where
    the puddles seep
and seep back out again in dripping springs and small dense
    copses, back out into the world—

I would press my palms into yours, the bear of my body, the very
    earth of me
I am unafraid to know you this way, to learn your life as part of
    mine.

Cameron Scott grew up on cinder cones, blackberry vines, rocky mountains, and ten thousand lakes. He spends most of his time standing in rivers, fighting currents he has no control over, in search of fish. If you have leftovers, he will eat them.